How To Star[t]

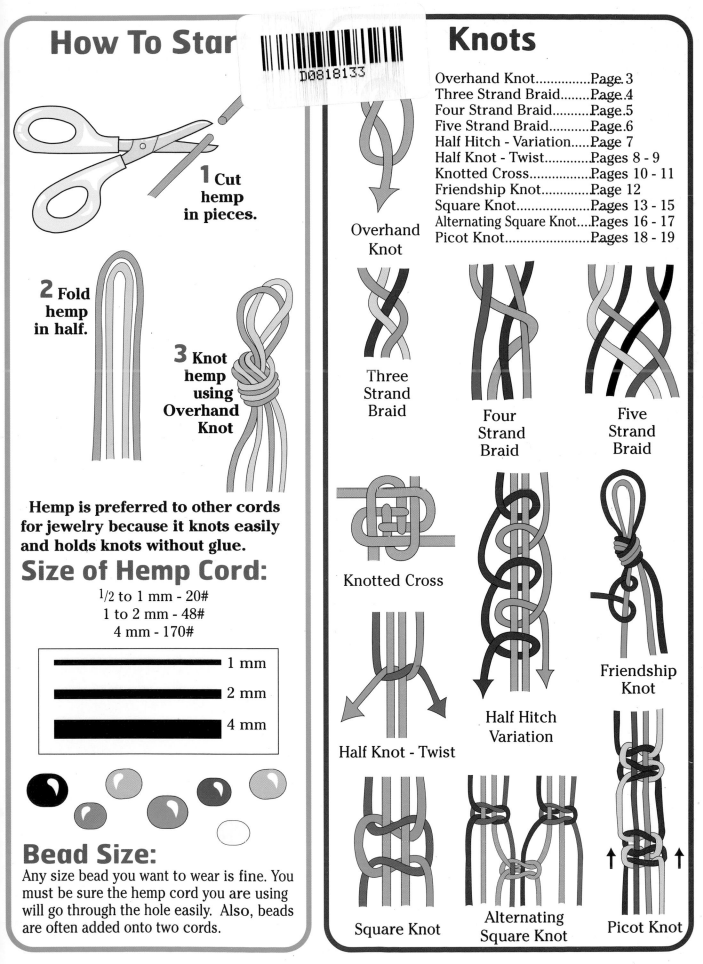

1 Cut hemp in pieces.

2 Fold hemp in half.

3 Knot hemp using Overhand Knot

Hemp is preferred to other cords for jewelry because it knots easily and holds knots without glue.

Size of Hemp Cord:

1/2 to 1 mm - 20#
1 to 2 mm - 48#
4 mm - 170#

1 mm
2 mm
4 mm

Bead Size:

Any size bead you want to wear is fine. You must be sure the hemp cord you are using will go through the hole easily. Also, beads are often added onto two cords.

Knots

Overhand Knot

Three Strand Braid

Four Strand Braid

Five Strand Braid

Knotted Cross

Half Knot - Twist

Half Hitch Variation

Friendship Knot

Square Knot

Alternating Square Knot

Picot Knot

Hooked on Hemp 3

Terms:

Add Beads - Always thread beads onto the filler cords, unless the instructions are different.

Fold Cord in Half - Find the center of the cord and fold it in half, so that both ends are the same length.

Knotting Cords - Longer cords will be used to tie the knots. Usually you will tie over/around filler cords. Bring knotting cords to the outside of the work after the beginning knot or end clamp is completed.

Filler Cords - Shorter cords you will knot around. Beads will usually be strung onto these cords.

Basic Tips:

Tightening Knots - For a strong ending knot, tighten each cord individually. If possible use pliers to pull cords tight for the ending knots.

Running out of cord - Sometimes you can switch the remaining filler cord with the knotting cord, and get a few more knots. Switching cords will show, so hide the change in a bead or in the middle of a knot, if possible.

Tacky Glue - Use Tacky glue to secure knots and ends.

How To Measure:

Knotting cords should be 5 to 6 times as long as the finished piece, if you are using close Square Knots or Half Knot Twist. The more spaces, or beads, the shorter the knotting cords can be. Also, if you knot tightly, you will need more cord, and if you knot loosely, you will not use up so much cord.

Tools:

Use Needlenose pliers to attach end clamps to jump rings.

 Correct way to open jump ring — side to side.

Incorrect way to open jump ring — opening ring wider.

Closures:

Jewelry Clasp: Attach end clamps such as 'squeeze clamps' to beginning and ending cords. Attach jump rings and/or eye rings to squeeze clamps.

Knot Clasp: Slip a large end knot through the beginning loop.

Three Strand Braid

Three Strand Green Bracelet with Bead

MATERIALS:
• One 22" piece of 1mm Green hemp
• One 44" pieces of 1mm Green hemp

INSTRUCTIONS:

1 Fold the 44" piece of cord in half, tie the 22" piece on to it, leaving a 1/2" loop.

2 Braid for 4"; add a bead. Braid for 4". Tie an Overhand Knot, trim the ends.

Meaning of Colors

Red — Love, passion, energy, enthusiasm, courage

Orange — Strength, authority, attraction, joy, success

Yellow — Clairvoyance, learning, mind, communication

Green — Healing, money, prosperity, luck, fertility

Blue — Meditation, healing, tranquility, forgiveness

Purple — Spirituality, wisdom, psychic awareness

White — Protection, peace, purity, truth

Pink — Emotional love, friendships, affection, harmony

Sea Green — Calming, emotional healing and protection

Rose — Self love, enhancing relationships

Black — Absorption and destruction of negative energy

Lavender — Intuition, dignity, spiritual shield

Peach — Gentle strength and joy

Turquoise — Awareness, meditation, moon, creativity

Four Strand Braid

Left — under 1 and back over 1

Right — under 2, in the center, and back over 1

Left — under 2, in the center, and back over 1

Right — under 2, in the center, and back over 1

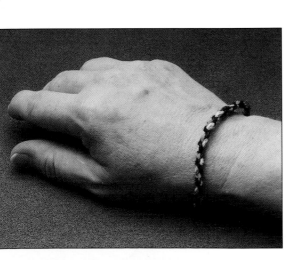

Four Strand Turquoise Bracelet

MATERIALS:
• One 22" piece each of 1mm hemp cord
   Turquoise, Red, Natural, Black

INSTRUCTIONS:

1 Tie all cords in an Overhand Knot. Braid in a 4-Strand Braid pattern for 10". Tie an Overhand Knot in the end of the braid, leaving a 1/2" loop. Trim the ends.

Five Strand Braid

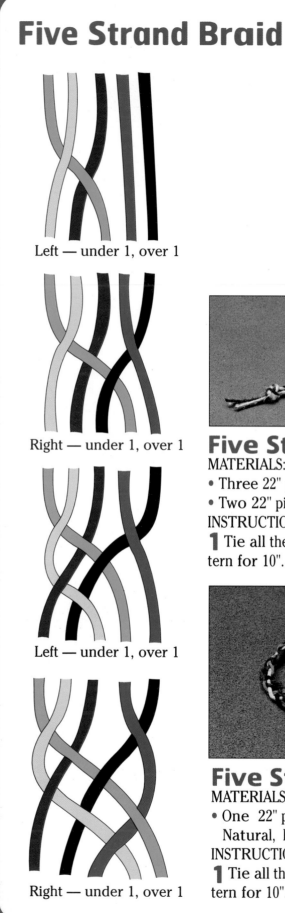

Left — under 1, over 1

Right — under 1, over 1

Left — under 1, over 1

Right — under 1, over 1

Five Strand Natural & Black Bracelet
MATERIALS:
• Three 22" pieces of 1mm Black hemp
• Two 22" pieces of 1mm Natural hemp
INSTRUCTIONS:
1 Tie all the cords in an Overhand Knot. Braid in a 5-Strand Brand pattern for 10". Tie an Overhand Knot, leaving a 3/4" loop. Trim the ends.

Five Strand Multi-Colored Bracelet
MATERIALS:
• One 22" piece each of 1mm hemp cord
   Natural, Black, Red, Turquoise, Navy
INSTRUCTIONS:
1 Tie all the cords in an Overhand Knot. Braid in a 5-Strand Braid pattern for 10". Tie an Overhand Knot, leaving a 3/4" loop. Trim the ends.

Half Hitch – Double Knot Variations

**1 Left
1 Right**

**2 Left
2 Right**

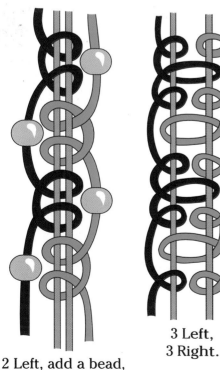

**2 Left, add a bead,
2 Right, add a bead.**

**3 Left,
3 Right.**

Red & Green Bracelet

MATERIALS:
- One 95" piece of 1mm Red hemp
- One 95" piece of 1mm Green hemp

INSTRUCTIONS:

1 Put ends of the cords together; fold them 14" from one end. Tie an Overhand Knot, leaving a 1/2" loop. The long pieces are knotting cords; the short pieces are filler cords.

2 With the Green knotting cord, tie a Half Hitch-Double Knot (2 Left, 2 Right) over both filler cords.

3 With the Red knotting cord, tie a Half Hitch-Double Knot (2 Left, 2 Right) over both filler cords. Continue this pattern to the end of the bracelet, alternating colors.

4 Tie a Double Overhand Knot (tie a second knot on top of the first knot). Trim the ends.

Navy & Turquoise Bracelet

MATERIALS:
- One 95" piece of 1mm Royal Blue hemp
- One 95" piece of 1mm Turquoise hemp

INSTRUCTIONS:
Repeat the instructions above using Blue and Turquoise colored cords.

Half Knot Twist

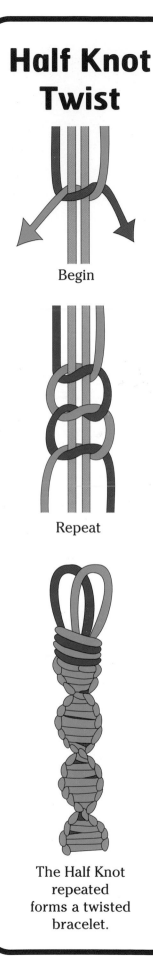

Begin

Repeat

The Half Knot repeated forms a twisted bracelet.

Purple Twist Bracelet

MATERIALS:
- One 100" piece of 1mm Purple hemp for knotting cord
- One 30" piece of 1mm Purple hemp for filler cord

INSTRUCTIONS:

1 Fold the cords in half; tie an Overhand Knot, leaving a 1/2" loop.

2 Tie a Half Knot-Twist for 8".

3 Tie a Double Overhand Knot (Tie a second knot on top of the first knot). Trim the ends.

Alpha Bead Twist Bracelet

MATERIALS:
- One 96" piece of 1mm Turquoise hemp
- One 96" piece of 1mm Royal Blue hemp
- One 3/8" round bead for closure
- Two 1/4" heart beads
- 1/4" Alphabet Beads for name

Note: The more alphabet beads used, the shorter the beginning and ending knotted sections will be. Each bead will take up about 1/4".

INSTRUCTIONS:

1 Fold the cords in half; tie an Overhand Knot, leaving a 1/2" loop. Separate the cords in this manner: 1 Blue cord for knotting cord and 1 for filler; 1 Turquoise cord for knotting cord and 1 for filler. Tie a Half Knot-Twist pattern for the beginning length of bracelet.

2 Begin the bead section: tie half of a Square Knot, add a heart bead, finish the Square Knot. Add name beads in the same manner. End with a heart bead.

3 Finish the bracelet length with the Half Knot-Twist pattern. Thread the round bead onto all cords; tie an Overhand Knot. Trim the ends.

Rainbow Clay Bead Bracelet

MATERIALS:
- One 100" piece of 1mm Turquoise hemp for knotting cord
- One 30" piece of 1mm Turquoise hemp for filler cord
- Three round multicolor Fimo beads 3/8"
- One multicolor tube shaped Fimo bead 1/2"

INSTRUCTIONS:

1 Fold the knotting cord in half. Attach the filler cord with an Overhand Knot, leaving a 3/4" loop.

2 Tie a Half Knot-Twist for 2 3/4". Add a round bead.

3 Tie a Half Knot-Twist for 3/4". Add the tube bead.

4 Tie a Half Knot-Twist for 3/4". Add a round bead.

5 Tie a Half Knot-Twist for 2 3/4". Tie an Overhand Knot. Add a round bead. Tie an Overhand Knot. Trim the ends.

Black Pendant Necklace with Large Bead

MATERIALS:
- Four 75" pieces of 1mm Black hemp for knotting cord
- Two 60" pieces of 1mm Black hemp for filler cord
- One large barrel shape striped bead
- Three 3/8" tube shaped orange beads

INSTRUCTIONS:

1 Line up the ends of the knotting cords; tie in an Overhand Knot. Trim the ends. Thread all cords through the large bead. Tie 1 Square Knot; do not tighten the last loop.

2 Thread the filler cords through the last loop of the Square Knot; even up ends. Tighten the Square Knot. Divide the cords into 2 groups.

3 With 1 group of cords, tie a Half Knot-Twist for 1 1/2". Add a small orange bead. Tie a Half Knot-Twist for 4". Tie 10 Square Knots. Repeat with the other group of cords.

4 On one end, thread a small orange bead onto all cords; tie an Overhand Knot. Trim the ends.

5 On the remaining end, separate the cords into 2 groups of 2 threads each. Tie an Overhand Knot in each group next to the last Square Knot. Leave a 1/2" space, tie all cords in an Overhand Knot. Trim the ends.

Knotted Cross

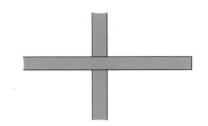

1 Cut four 36" pieces of hemp for each cross.

Lay 1 piece vertically.

Lay 1 strand horizontally across the first one, crossing strands at the center.

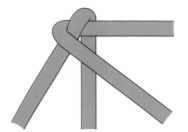

2 Fold vertical strand down at an angle over the horizontal strand.

Fold the left end of the horizontal strand over.

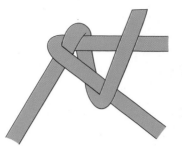

3 Fold the bottom of the vertical strand up at an angle.

4 Fold the right end of the horizontal strand over and through the loop formed by the first fold in Step 2.

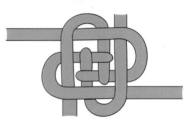

5 The First knot at the end of one cross arm is completed. Make another knot on top of the first knot. Tie 8 more knots, for a total of 10 knots for each arm of the cross.

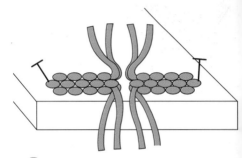

6 Repeat Steps 1- 5 with other 2 strands of hemp to make the other arm.

Pin ends of arms to a foam block.

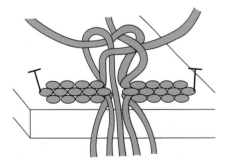

7 For the bottom of cross, use 1 cord from each arm. The cross bottom has 22 knots. Secure the last knot with a dab of glue, and trim the ends close when dry. Dot ends with glue again to prevent ravels.

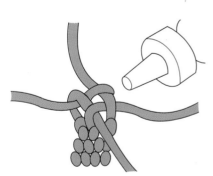

8 Tie 10 knots for the top of the cross with the remaining strands above the arms. Glue the last knot. Tie the ends with an Overhand Knot into a 1/2" loop to be threaded onto the necklace.

Red Knotted Cross

MATERIALS:
- Four 36" pieces of 1mm Red hemp for cross
- One 200" piece of 1mm Red hemp for necklace knotting cord
- One 40" piece of 1mm Red hemp for necklace filler cord

INSTRUCTIONS FOR CROSS:
Follow steps on page 10.

INSTRUCTIONS FOR NECKLACE:

1 Fold the cords in half; tie an Overhand Knot, leaving a 1/2" loop. Tie a Half Knot-Twist pattern for 16 1/2", or the length desired.

2 Tie a Double Overhand Knot (tie a second knot on top of the first knot). Trim the ends. Thread the end of the necklace through the loop on top of the cross.

Friendship Knotting

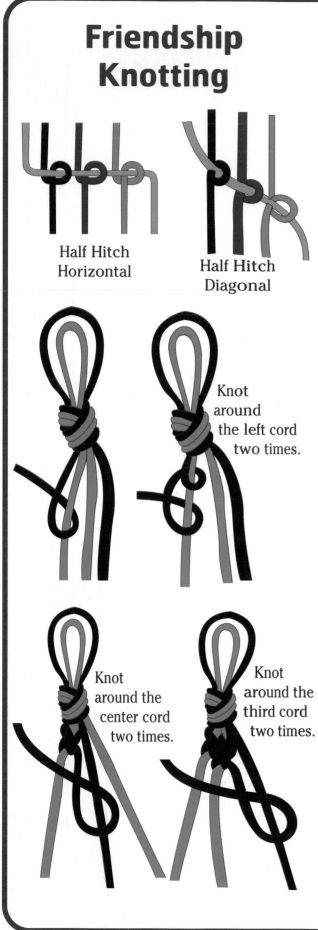

Half Hitch
Horizontal

Half Hitch
Diagonal

Knot
around
the left cord
two times.

Knot
around the
center cord
two times.

Knot
around the
third cord
two times.

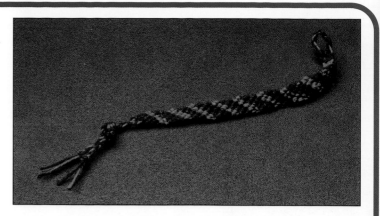

Red, Turquoise & Purple Bracelet
MATERIALS:
• Three 110" pieces of 1mm hemp cord
  1 each of Red, Turquoise, Purple
INSTRUCTIONS:
1 Find the center of cords; braid the 3 cords together for 2". Tie an Overhand Knot, leaving a $1/2$" loop. Arrange the colors left to right: 2 Purple, 2 Red, 2 Turquoise.
2 Using the first Purple cord on the left, tie the Friendship Knot across the remaining cords. Continue tying knots, left to right, following the color sequence for 5 $1/2$".
3 Separate the cords into 2 groups; braid each group for 4", tie an Overhand Knot. Trim the ends.

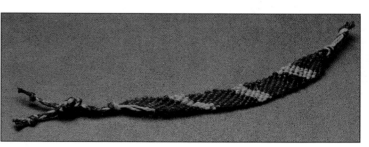

Red, Turquoise & Blue Bracelet
MATERIALS:
• Four 55" pieces of 1mm Red hemp
• Two 55" pieces of 1mm Turquoise hemp
• Two 55" pieces of 1mm Navy hemp
INSTRUCTIONS:
1 Put the ends of the cords together, tie an Overhand Knot. Leave a $3/4$" space then tie an Overhand Knot. Arrange colors left to right: 4 Red, 2 Turquoise, 2 Navy.
2 Using the first Red cord on the left, tie Friendship Knots across the remaining cords. Continue tying knots, left to right, following the color sequence for 5 $1/2$".
3 Separate the cords into 2 groups; braid each group for 4", tie an Overhand Knot. Trim the ends.

Square Knot

continued on page 14

Part 1

Part 2

Sinnet
or
series
of Square Knots

Turquoise Bracelet with Red Filler Cord

MATERIALS:
• One 84" piece of 1mm Turquoise hemp for knotting cord
• One 25" piece of 1mm Red hemp for filler cord

INSTRUCTIONS:

1 Fold the cords in half; tie an Overhand Knot, leaving a 1/2" loop.

2 Tie 42 Square Knots. Finish with a Double Overhand Knot (tie a second knot on top of the first knot). Trim the ends.

Square Knot continued from page 13

Red & Navy Bracelet

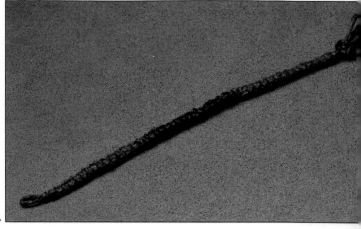

MATERIALS:
- One 60" piece of 1mm Red hemp
- One 40" piece of 1mm Navy hemp

INSTRUCTIONS:

1 Fold the Navy cord in half. Attach the Red cord with an Overhand Knot, leaving a 1/2" loop. Using the Red cord as a knotting cord, tie 14 Square Knots.

2 Put the Red cords in the center for filler cords. Tie 14 Square Knots with the Navy cord.

3 Put the Navy cords in the center for filler cords.

4 Tie 14 Square Knots with Red cord.

Tie a Double Overhand Knot (tie a second knot on top of first knot) with all the cords. Trim the ends.

Turquoise & Black Bracelet with Spaces

MATERIALS:
- One 80" piece of 1mm Turquoise hemp for knotting cord
- One 24" piece of 1mm Black hemp for filler cord

INSTRUCTIONS:

1 Fold the Turquoise cord in half; attach the Black cord with an Overhand Knot. Tie 5 Square Knots. Leave a 1" space. Repeat until you have 4 spaces, ending with 5 Square Knots.

2 Tie all cords in a Double Overhand Knot (tie a second knot on top of first knot). Trim the ends.

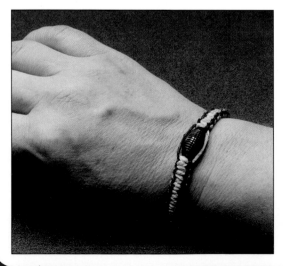

Natural & Green Bracelet

MATERIALS:
- One 60" piece of 2mm Natural hemp
- One 60" piece of 1mm Green hemp
- One 1/2" Green bead

INSTRUCTIONS:

1 Put the ends of cords together. At a point 15" from the ends, tie an Overhand Knot, leaving a 1/2" loop. You will have one Green and one Natural knotting cord (the long pieces), and one Green and one Natural filler cord (the short pieces).

2 Tie 19 Square Knots. Add a bead. Tie 19 Square Knots.

3 Tie a Double Overhand Knot with all cords. Trim the ends.

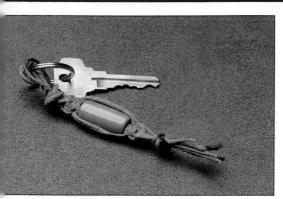

Turquoise Key Ring
MATERIALS:
- Two 12" pieces of 1mm Turquoise hemp
- Two 10" pieces of 1mm Purple hemp
- 25mm Split Key Ring

INSTRUCTIONS:

1 Fold the cords in half; tie an Overhand knot, leaving a 1/4" loop. Tie 2 Square Knots. Add a bead. Tie 2 Square Knots.
2 Tie an Overhand Knot. Trim the ends. Attach to a Key Ring.

Purple Necklace with White Beads
MATERIALS:
- One 140" piece of 1mm Purple hemp for knotting cord
- One 30" piece of 1mm Purple hemp for filler cord
- Six White 1/4" tube beads
- Two 1" White tube beads

INSTRUCTIONS:

1 Fold the cords in half; tie an Overhand Knot, leaving a 1/2" loop. Tie 5 Square Knots; add a small bead. Repeat 2 times (3 beads added).
2 Tie 3 Square Knots. Add a long bead. Tie 3 Square Knots.
3 Tie 5 Square Knots; add a small bead. Repeat 2 times (3 beads added).
4 Tie 19 Square Knots; add a long bead. Tie an Overhand Knot. Trim the ends.

Green Cross Necklace
MATERIALS:
- Two 108" pieces of 1mm Green hemp for knotting cord
- Two 76" pieces of 1mm Green hemp for filler cord
- One Green cross bead
- Three glass 1/4" Natural Pony beads
- One round 1/2" Natural glass bead

INSTRUCTIONS:

1 Center one pony bead on the two 108" pieces of hemp. Tie 4 Square Knots. Add the cross bead. Tie 6 Square Knots. Do not tighten the last loop of the last Square Knot.
2 Thread the 76" cords through the back loop of the Square Knot, center cords. Tighten the Square Knot.
3 Divide cords into two groups; the longer cords are knotting cords; the shorter cords are filler cords. With one group of cords, tie 5 Square Knots. Add a pony bead over all the cords. Tie 33 Square Knots. Repeat with the other group of cords.

4 On one end, separate cords into two groups of two cords. Tie an Overhand Knot with each group. Leave a 1/2" space, tie all cords into an Overhand Knot.
5 On the other end, thread a round bead onto all the cords; tie an Overhand Knot. Trim the ends.

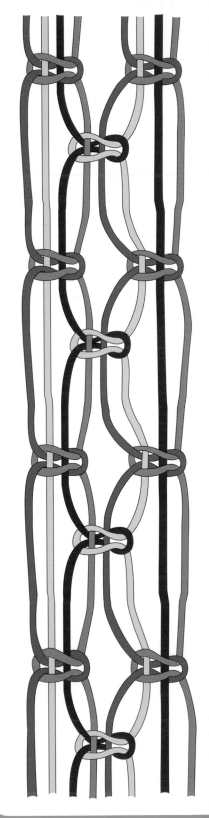

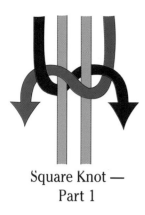

Square Knot —
Part 1

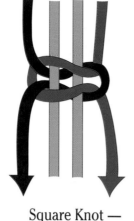

Square Knot —
Part 2

Multi-color Choker
MATERIALS:
- Two 95" pieces of 1mm Red hemp
- One 95" piece of 1mm Navy hemp
- One 95" piece of 1mm Purple hemp

INSTRUCTIONS:

1 Fold the cords in half; tie an Overhand Knot, leaving a 1/2" loop. Separate cords into two groups: One will have two Purple cords for knotting cords, and two of Red cords for filler cord. The other group will have two Navy cords for knotting cords, and the other two Red cords for filler cord.

2 Tie the Alternating Square Knot pattern for 13". Tie all the cords in a Double Overhand Knot (tie a second knot on top of the first knot). Trim the ends.

Natural & Green Bracelet
MATERIALS:
- Two 90" pieces of 1mm Natural hemp cord
- Two 90" pieces of 1mm Green hemp cord
- Two 1/2" long Natural tube beads

INSTRUCTIONS:

1 Fold the cords in half; tie an Overhand Knot, leaving a 1/2" loop. Separate cords into two groups of four: in each group, use two Natural cords for knotting cords, and two Green cords as filler cords.

2 Tie the Alternating Square Knot pattern for 3".

3 Tie 3 Square Knots with the center cords, then add a bead to the two outer cords.

4 Tie the Alternating Square Knot pattern for 3".

5 Finish with a Double Overhand Knot (tie a second knot on top of the first knot). Trim the ends.

Square Knot / Half Knot

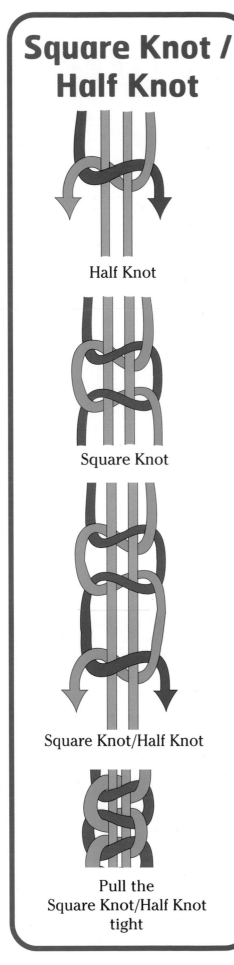

Half Knot

Square Knot

Square Knot/Half Knot

Pull the
Square Knot/Half Knot
tight

Picot Knot

Picot Knot
Variation

Tie 1
Square Knot,
then tie 1
Half Knot,
then skip 1"
to the next set
of knots to
complete
each section
between the
Picots.

After tying the second section of knots,
push the bottom knot up next to the top
knot to create loops or Picots.